GW00724945

DEGAS

DEGAS

PAINTINGS

Introduction by
Lara Vinca Masini

Geddes & Grosset

Translated by Christopher Clark
Edited and adapted by Colin Clark

First published 1980
© 1980 Nardini Editore, Centro
Internazionale del Libro SpA, Florence,
Italy
© 1980 Giunti Marzocco SpA, Florence,
Italy
First published in this edition 1990
Published by Geddes & Grosset Ltd,
David Dale House,
New Lanark, Scotland
© Geddes & Grosset Ltd

ISBN 1-85534 010 0

Printed in Yugoslavia

CONTENTS

	Page
Introduction	7
Biographical details	27
The paintings	33
Geographical index of paintings	147
Title index of paintings	153

Degas

'Art is vice,' Edgar Degas once said, 'you don't marry it legally, you rape it.' The figure of Degas (during his early working years he still signed with his aristocratic family's name, De Gas) is generally associated with the major exponents of the Impressionist movement. Nevertheless, he moved on to occupy a special place on the French artistic scene in the second half of the nineteenth century, both for the originality of his experimentation and for his individual interpretation of Impressionist rules.

The first of the rules that he broke was the one which made the artist merely the conductor of an impression, the means by which it was captured. For Degas, an impression was above all a moment of tension, an intellectual fact, lucid, aware and voluntarily provoked. He wrote, 'There has never been a less spontaneous art than mine. What I do is the result of reflection and study of the masters. Of inspiration, spontaneity and temperament, I know absolutely nothing.'

As far as Degas was concerned, it was thought, with its theoretical, practical capabilities, that controlled impression and, as a result, organized the space in an image. This space was shaped not according to the theories of classical perspective but by the elements within it, by a figure opening their arms or taking a step, or by the relationship between a figure or an object and the one next to it. It is no longer abstract, geometrical space, but an involving and involved space of movement, a foretaste of what Le Corbusier's modular would be in terms of architectural space.

It was gesture and movement that would create the new dimension of space in the image, an image in which the artist would be immersed. The artist was no longer someone who looked on and registered the scene from outside, but one who lived it from within, or at least from very close, and from above, below or alongside. 'No one,' he said, 'has ever painted monuments or houses from below, from underneath, from alongside, the way we see them when we pass along the street.' The effect is almost cinematic, echoing the various ways a film is shot: in close-up, from middle distance, in long shot, often all together in a single scene, as if several cameras are running together but from different angles in relation to the scene.

For this reason, Degas rejected the *plein air* approach of the Impressionists, their abandonment to the all-encompassing force of Nature. 'The study of nature,' in his words, 'is insignificant because painting is an art of convention. It would be much more worthwhile learning to draw from Holbein.' Except, therefore, for a series of solitary landscapes that are vague and hazy in tone, as if drawn from memory, and date from a visit Degas made to stay with Manet in Boulogne in 1869, when his subjects are out of doors, as in his racecourse scenes with horses and jockeys, Degas manages to catch the image as if through a lens, almost as if he had zoomed in close to the scene so that the details stand out clearly. Or else he gives the privacy of an indoor setting to an outdoor subject by fashioning an 'English' scene, with family carriages, or ladies holding umbrellas, or a coachman in a top hat, or a little dog.

Degas reached this point deliberately. He began by studying the old masters and the academic classicism of Ingres. When the two painters met, Ingres had said to the young Degas, 'Draw lines, young man, lots of lines, either from memory or from nature. That is how you will become a good artist.' Probably influenced by the work of the influential French photographer and writer, Nadar (whose studio, incidentally, housed the first two Impressionist exhibitions in 1874 and 1876), Degas also analysed the possibilities offered by photography as a tool for composing scenes. The technology of the new medium meant it was no longer, or not only, confined to portraying a posed scene, like a daguerrotype imitating a portrait. Now it was a means of capturing an image in a different way and of fixing moments that the speed of movement renders too fast for conscious visual perception. Eadweard Muybridge's photographic recording of horses in motion had first been drawn to the attention of the French art world in 1878, and by the time his zoopraxiscope for projecting animated images was first demonstrated in Paris in 1888, Degas had already made use in his paintings of the insights offered by photography, analysing the moment's impression through that basic factor of photography, light, which in its turn vibrated with colour.

By looking at Degas's history works,

from *Young Spartans* (London, National Gallery) with its triangular composition, its top-heavy emphasis on the arms of the groups in the foreground, and with the linear background interrupted in the middle by the costumed group of mothers, to *Semiramis building Babylon* (Paris), we can see the effect of his study of the old masters, although rendered with a contemporary vision of the image.

Degas was particularly influenced by the Florentine painters of the fourteenth and fifteenth centuries, the Mannerists, especially Jacopo Pontormo for his nightmarish transfigurations, the timbre of his painting, and, perhaps, his search for special optical effects, although Degas did not tend to deform the image in his portrayal of dynamic tension. In details, he was probably influenced by the work of Antonio Pollaiuolo in studying movement. The boys and girls of *Young Spartans* are not based on classical models but are stereotypes of nineteenth-century youths. With their slender bodies, the intense sharpness of their facial expressions, they bring to mind the image that was to be created years later in the acrobats of Picasso's blue period.

Even the group of figures in *Semiramis building Babylon* can be seen as an echo of the fourteenth-century Florentine painters, where the medieval, classically influenced content of the scene does not exclude a stylistic relationship to certain Pre-Raphaelite compositions, without, however, the revivalist purpose of the Pre-Raphaelites.

Degas's transition to the contemporary style of the nineteenth century took place through a series of portraits which heralded a new, more direct concentration on the subject's emotional responses, delineated by movement, point of view and light. Even here, he was influenced by the old masters, by Ingres, but, most of all, by character details from Flemish painters, from Holbein to Clouet, who 'made use of all sorts of objects laid out and combined in such a way that they are impregnated with the life of a man or a woman; newly removed corsets, for example, which still hold the shape of a body.'

In his brilliant portrait of *The Bellelli family* (Paris), his study of the ancient masters is transformed. Painted from a series of sketches made during a stay in Naples with relatives, even the beautiful pyramidal shape of his aunt, the Baroness Bellelli, reminiscent of the almost dome-like architectural forms of the Madonnas painted by the Florentine, Masaccio, portrays an amazing awareness of modern existential problems in the subtle sharpness of the elongated face. In this painting, the images are not symbols but rather beacons of psychological tension, pointing up the whole scene, from the image of the baroness whose position indicates her status as ruler, to that of the baron, viewed from the side and behind at the right of the painting, to the other small, central figures of the daughters, one of whom has her leg drawn up under her skirt. Apart from the non-traditional positioning of this family group, the painting is also interesting for the use of black in strong contrast to white. This was a frequent and anti-Impressionist characteristic of Degas. The space surrounding the figures is laid out harmoniously, the walls, paintings and table at the same time creating and negating illusions of depth in the already unbalanced setting of the composition — 'the famous and cursed outstanding features', as the art historian Longhi described such ordinary objects.

Degas has already acquired that 'indoor poetry' that was later also to characterize Edouard Vuillard, who, however, interpreted it in a different way. For Degas, the human figure is surrounded by space, defined by its possibilities of movement, from that of the eye, to the footstep, to the relationship between figures, and between figures and objects, which he filters through light. In Vuillard's work, the human body is lost on the flat space of the canvas and plays no more than a decorative role.

In the first of Degas's two self-portraits (Paris), he conveys an acute sense of introspection, revealing the worry and introversion as well as a pitiless awareness of his own character. In the second (Lisbon), the self-portrait is more extravert and worldly, encapsulating Degas's rejection of things Bohemian. Nevertheless, in the melancholy expression it catches a sensitive light in the eye. The influence of Ingres is obvious here in the clear outline of the image and the dense colour tones.

In the portrait of his brother, *Achille De Gas in the uniform of a cadet* (Washington DC, National Gallery), the clean, dark-coloured surround, the accurately composed drawing and the chromatic juxtaposition reveal a direct, sensitive and involved relationship between the artist and his subject, a relationship caught also in the expression on the face and the naturalness of the pose.

It was not by chance that most of the subjects of Degas's early portraits belonged to his family and to a high social position. His merciless eye was later to turn towards individuals from other classes: dancers, both on stage and the ones waiting behind the scenes, poorly paid and often swiftly sacked, to substitute for the top dancers; laundresses; singers; the women who frequented cafés. To Degas they were almost like guinea pigs, of no real significance as individuals but of use as expressions of the human and social situations in which they are almost unwittingly involved.

Even *Head of a young woman* (Paris) is probably the portrait of a relative. The sensitive luminous refinement of the face, the delicate intensity of the expression, the soft touch in the range of colour, result in a particularly intense note to this portrait, which he rarely reached in other portraits.

Degas also painted the lovely *Hortense Valpinçon* (Minneapolis), probably during a trip to Normandy in 1869 to stay with his friends, the Valpinçon family. This is an excellent example of an indoor setting, with the clear-cut and delicately defined figure of the little girl standing out against the soft, almost dreamy, flower background that repeats, in a lighter shade, the pattern of flowers in the foreground. Here we can see how differently Degas deals with the relationship and the contrast, compared to some later indoor scenes by Vuillard.

Between 1862 and 1872, Degas painted the portrait of *Marie Dihau at the piano* (Paris), into which he introduced a musical reference, the white rectangle of the score acting as a contrast to the low colour of the rest. And then there is the *Woman with chrysanthemums* (New York), where the foreground is entirely taken up with a huge mass of flowers and the portrait is confined to the far right. Another fine example of an indoor setting is *A pedicure* (Paris), where the girl is wrapped in a white bathrobe and leans back against a sofa, surrounded by the personal objects of a bourgeois household. And in *Interior* (Philadelphia), Degas seems to anticipate Expressionist motifs similar to those used by the Norwegian painter, Edvard Munch.

In 1869, Degas painted the double portrait, *Pagans and Auguste De Gas* (Paris). He often sought a psychological contrast between two images. Here, the erect figure of the singer is clearly opposed to the bent, intent, almost humble figure of Degas's elderly father whose sensitive head, bowed as he listens to the music, stands out against the white rectangle of the score. His clasped hands move out of the picture to the right, where clashes of colour bear witness to emotional intensity.

The musical theme was much used by Degas for the emotional definition of his characters, as in his many portraits of musicians, such as *The orchestra of the*

Opéra, The cellist Pillet (both in Paris), and *Musicians in the orchestra* (Frankfurt), and where originally it was merely a background for such paintings, the ballet was to become one of Degas's major themes. It was also to be a sign of a new direction in his painting, for it marked quite clearly the transfer of his attention towards scenes from life. With this move he passed from the soft filtered light of private indoor scenes to the harsh glaring spotlight of public performance, a light that falsifies and distorts surroundings, that eliminates the intimate in favour of the public. Colours break down and blend together and flash out blindingly, leaving little room for the psychological dimension.

Degas's painting technique changes as well. From using a clear incisive coherent outline, he passes on to 'a feathery and all-encompassing flow of masses, mixed in a luminous space but still expressed in basic movements', as F. Russoli has written. The new style brings to mind the airy 'gesturalism' of his Italian contemporary, Giovanni Boldini, except that in Boldini's work it is the brushstroke that creates the gesture, whereas in Degas's it is the light that, almost automatically, flows on to the pigmentation.

Degas moved on from the use of oils to the use of pastel and monotype, a method of producing a print by painting on copper. He also adopted highly varied viewpoints which focus on scenes from almost unnatural angles. Dancers in white frothy dresses ('the muslin of Degas with no outline,' as Longhi put it) are caught in all their ordinary movements against backgrounds that become more and more rarefied, bathed in light — *Rehearsal of the ballet on stage* (Paris), *Two dancers on stage* (London, Courtauld Institute), *Dancer with a bouquet* and *L'Etoile* (both in Paris). A detail in the foreground, such as a foot or a fan, as in *Dancer with a bouquet, seen from a loge* (Providence, Rhode Island) leads us into the scene and suggests depth without mass.

It is still the gesture that counts. The faces disappear into anonimity.

Meanwhile, a soft, gentle indoor feeling returns in some paintings, like *Monsieur Perrot's dance class* (Paris), where the summer light of late afternoon filters in through long windows and almost sleepily comes to rest in soft shadows on the wooden floor.

In his scene set in a cafe, *Absinthe* (Paris), we find a direct reference to Japanese prints in the warped perspective created by directional lines in the space around the figure. But the tired resigned face of the woman shows a profound analysis of the human condition. There is analysis also in the close-up in *Café-concert singer wearing a glove* (Cambridge, Mass.). Here Degas is showing us a slice of life with a realism as bitter as any in the writings of Balzac or Zola, although for Degas this is still only a pretext for capturing images in their moment of greatest tension.

It is the gestures and movements of the women that attract his attention in *Women ironing* (Paris). The air is steamy from the heat of the iron flourished by the strong arms of the two women who move it methodically and repetitively over the clothes, their yawns showing their boredom, or their weariness.

Degas's touch has become more nervous and rapid, showing a foretaste of post-Impressionist pointillism. It can be seen in his thick vibrant strokes, creating colour out of the breakdown of light. In his pictures of nudes, he records intimate actions, like women bathing, stretching, drying themselves, combing their hair, almost 'as if they were being seen through a keyhole,' as he said himself. Degas has translated movement into a synthesis of colour and shape. His female nudes are not viewed with the hint of eroticism or emotion that Renoir brought to his, but as objects of study, a reason for analysing movement and the reactions of light and colour at various dynamic moments. His attention has returned to indoor scenes, but no longer those of the wealthy. Instead, harsh lonely environments are painted, with a hint of desolation and squalor: unmade beds, zinc tubs, bits of curtaining, hinting at impossible dreams of comfort and luxury. The figures are executed with rapid lines, full of colour, creating wells of blue and green, contrasting with pink in a thousand shades.

Meanwhile, Degas, who was by nature a solitary character and not fond of socialising, was becoming more and more closed in on himself, living in the centre of Paris but in a gloomy, hypochondriacal solitude. Edouard Manet, with whom he had a strange love-hate relationship, died in 1883. But Degas was careful to keep up his reputation as someone impossible to deal with. When he heard that a model was reporting that he was not as grumpy as he appeared to be, he exclaimed, 'Tell her to stop! She'll ruin my reputation!' Worst of all, he was losing his eyesight and painting, even in pastel, was becoming more and more difficult for him. This explains why, towards the end of his life, he spent more time on sculpture which earlier he had practised only occasionally but which also represented proof of his concept of space.

The subjects of his sculptures were again horses, shown jumping or galloping, light and finely wrought; dancers, as in *Grande arabesque, third position* (Paris); and women generally, as in *The tub,* (Berne). He made *Little dancer of fourteen years* (New York) in wax and dressed it in a dress of real linen and muslin, with waxed shoes, almost in anticipation of the collages of the future or the hardened waxes used by the Dadaists. In his sculptures, Degas also shows that he was influenced by Renaissance sculptors. There is a direct link between the stance of the *Little dancer* and the *David* by Verrocchio and its predecessor, the bronze *David* by Donatello. There is the same light uneven unstable balance and the same indolent slenderness. The difference is in the treatment of the polished surfaces that shine softly in the sliding touch of light in Verrocchio and Donatello but are harsh and vibrant in Degas's work, as if to multiply the possibilities for reactions to light. We should consider how much twentieth-century sculpture owes to these works by Degas, as much as to Rodin or others.

Perhaps the best way to end this short introduction to Degas is with one of the verses he dedicated to dance, which reveals his almost scientific purpose:

'In nothing, as always, the great mystery ends.
She bends her legs backwards, too far, in a leap.
It is the leap of a frog in Cytherea's pond.'

Biographical details

1834   July 19 — Hilaire Germain Edgar De Gas is born in Paris, the son of Pierre August Hyacinthe De Gas, a nobleman of Breton origin and a bank director, and of Celestine Musson, from a Creole family, originally from New Orleans.

1845   Edgar attends the Lycée Louis-le-Grand in Paris, where he is taught drawing.

1853   Having obtained his *baccalaureat*, he enters the studio of the painter Félix Barrias and begins spending a lot of time in the Louvre and other museums, studying the old masters.

1855	April — he becomes a pupil of Louis Lamothe, a disciple of Ingres, at the Ecoles des Beaux Arts. He soon leaves, but he has met Ingres.
1856	October — he begins a ten-month study period in Rome.
1857	He travels to Naples, where he stays with his grandfather, René-Hilaire De Gas.
1858	In Paris, he begins to take an interest in Japanese prints. He returns to Italy, studies in Florence and Siena and spends time with the Macchiaioli group of painters based in Tuscany.
1859	Travels in Italy then settles in Paris and begins his period of history painting.
1860	Visits Italy. Begins his interest in horses and racecourses.
1862	Enters the circle of the future Impressionists.
1865	Exhibits at the Salon for the first time.

1870	During the Siege of Paris in the course of the Franco-Prussian War, he serves in the artillery.
1872	October — he sets off with his brother, René, for New Orleans to visit relatives of his mother.
1873	Returns from New Orleans. Travels to Turin in Italy to be with his ailing father.
1874	February 23 — his father dies. April-May — he takes part in the first Impressionist exhibition in Paris, held at the studio of the photographer, Nadar. He exhibits ten works.
1875	Visits Italy.
1876	Shows more than twenty works at the second Impressionist exhibition.
1877	At the third Impressionist exhibition he again shows more than twenty works.
1879	He shows twenty-five works at the fourth Impressionist exhibition.

1880   He shows eight paintings and pastels at the fifth Impressionist exhibition.

1881   At the sixth Impressionist exhibition he shows seven pictures and his sculpture of the *Little dancer of fourteen years,* his only sculpture to be publicly exhibited during his lifetime. He is perfecting his monotype technique.

1882   Submits nothing to the seventh Impressionist exhibition.

1883   Death of Edouard Manet. From now on Degas grows steadily more isolated and his problems with his eyesight increase.

1886   Visits Naples. Exhibits fifteen works in the eighth and last Impressionist exhibition.

1889   September — travels with Giovanni Boldini to Spain and Morocco.

1890   Moves his home and studio to the Rue Victor Massé. Experiments with photography and augments his collection of works by other artists, including Ingres, Daumier, Manet, Pissarro, Cézanne, Gauguin and Van Gogh.

1892   Has his only one-man exhibition at the Durand-Ruel Gallery in Paris. It is an exhibition of monotype works.

1912   Degas has to leave his home and studio in Rue Victor Massé and move to the Boulevard de Clichy. Ever more alone and almost blind, he works more and more on sculptures and devotes himself to his private collection.

1917   September 27 — Degas dies. His funeral is attended by many from the Paris art world.

THE PAINTINGS

*Young Spartans ('Petites filles Spartiates
provoquant des garçons'), c.1860.*
Oil on canvas, 109 × 154 cm
(43 × 60¾ in).
London, National Gallery.

Semiramis building Babylon and detail (overleaf),
*c.*1861.
Oil on canvas, 151 × 258 cm (59½ × 101½ in).
Paris, Musée d'Orsay.

Self-portrait with pencil 1854-1855.
Oil on canvas, 81 × 64 cm
(31⁷/₈ × 25¹/₄ in).
Paris. Musée d'Orsay.

Achille De Gas in the uniform of a cadet 1856-1857.
Oil on canvas, 64 × 51 cm (25¼ × 20 in).
Washington, National Gallery of Art.

Self-portrait saluting 1863-1865.
Oil on canvas, 91 × 72 cm (35⅞ × 28⅜ in).
Lisbon, Calouste Gulbenkian Foundation.

The Bellelli family and detail (overleaf), 1859-1860.
Oil on canvas, 200 × 253 cm (78³/₄ × 98¹/₂ in).
Paris, Musée d'Orsay.

*Jockeys in front of the grandstands c.*1872.
Thinned oil on canvas, 46 × 61 cm
(18¹⁄₈ × 24 in).
Paris, Musée d'Orsay.

Woman with chrysanthemums 1865.
Oil on canvas, 74 × 92 cm (29⅛ × 36¼ in).

New York, Metropolitan Museum of
Art.

Above: *Head of a young woman* 1867.
Oil on canvas, 27 × 22 cm
(10⅝ × 8⅝ in).
Paris, Musée d'Orsay.

Opposite: *Pagans and Auguste De Gas* and detail
(overleaf), *c.*1869.
Oil on canvas, 54 × 39 cm
(21¼ × 15⅜ in).
Paris, Musée d'Orsay.

Hortense Valpinçon 1871.
Oil on canvas, 73 × 110 cm (28³/₄ × 43¹/₄ in).
Minneapolis, Institute of Arts.

Marie Dihau at the piano, c.1869-1872.
Oil on canvas, 45 × 32 cm
(17¾ × 12⅝ in).
Paris, Musée d'Orsay.

The orchestra of the Opéra and detail
(overleaf), 1868-1869.
Oil on canvas, 56.5 × 46 cm
(22¼ × 18⅛ in).
Paris, Musée d'Orsay.

The cellist Pillet 1868-1869.
Oil on canvas, 48 × 60 cm

$(18^7/_8 \times 23^5/_8$ in).
Paris, Musée d'Orsay.

Musicians in the orchestra and details
(opposite and overleaf), *c*.1872.
Oil on canvas, 69 × 49 cm
(27$\frac{1}{8}$ × 19$\frac{1}{4}$ in).
Frankfurt, Städelsches Kunstinstitut.

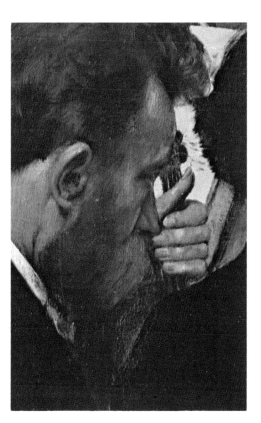

The dance lesson and detail (overleaf),
1872.
Oil on canvas, 32 × 46 cm
(12⅝ × 18⅛ in).
Paris, Musée d'Orsay.

Above: *A woman with a vase* 1872.
Oil on canvas, 65 × 54 cm
(25½ × 21¼ in).
Paris, Musée d'Orsay.

Opposite: *A pedicure* and detail (overleaf), 1873.
Thinned oil on board, 61 × 46 cm
(24 × 18⅛ in).
Paris, Musée d'Orsay.

Interior 1868-1869.
Oil on canvas, 81 × 116 cm
(31⅞ × 45⅝ in).
Philadelphia, Henry P. McIlhenny
Collection.

At the stock exchange 1879.
Oil on canvas, 100 × 82 cm (39³⁄₈ × 32¹⁄₄ in).
Paris, Musée d'Orsay.

Madame Jeantaud at a mirror and detail
(overleaf), 1875.
Oil on canvas, 70 × 84 cm
(27¹/₂ × 33 in).
Whereabouts unknown.

Absinthe and details (opposite, overleaf
and pages 84-85), *c.*1876.
Oil on canvas, 92 × 68 cm
(36¼ × 26¾ in).
Paris, Musée d'Orsay.

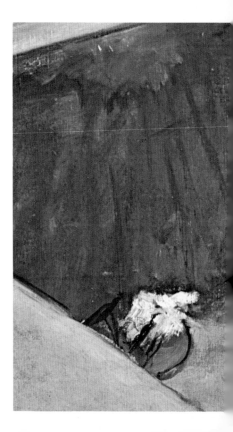

At the races, gentlemen jockeys 1877-1880.
Oil on canvas, 66 × 82 cm

(26 × 32¼ in).
Paris, Musée d'Orsay.

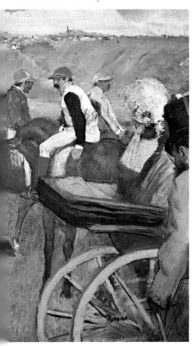

The café-concert at Les Ambassadeurs,
c.1876.
Pastel over monotype, 37 × 27 cm
(14½ × 10⅝ in).
Lyons, Musée des Beaux-Arts.

Café-concert singer wearing a glove,
*c.*1878.
Pastel on canvas, 53 × 41 cm
(20⁷⁄₈ × 16¹⁄₈ in).
Cambridge, Mass, Fogg Art Museum,
Harvard University.

Rehearsal of the ballet on stage and details (opposite and overleaf), 1874.
Thinned oil on canvas, 66 × 82 cm (26 × 32$^1/_1$ in)
Paris, Musée d'Orsay.

Two dancers on stage and detail
(opposite), 1874.
Pastel on paper, 62 × 46 cm
(24³⁄₈ × 18¹⁄₈ in).
London, Courtauld Institute.

Monsieur Perrot's dance class and details
(opposite and overleaf), *c.*1875.
Oil on canvas, 85 × 74 cm (33^1/$_2$ × 29^1/$_8$ in).
Paris, Musée d'Orsay.

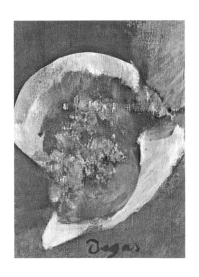

End of an arabesque and details (above and
overleaf), *c.*1877.
Thinned oil and pastel on canvas,
67 × 38 cm (26⅞ × 15 in).
Paris, Musée d'Orsay.

Dancer with bouquet of flowers and details (opposite and overleaf), *c.*1878.
Pastel on board on canvas.
Paris, Musée d'Orsay.

Above: *Dancer with a bouquet, seen from a loge, c.1878.*
Pastel and mixed media over monotype, 40 × 50 cm (15³/₄ × 19⁵/₈ in).
Providence, Rhode Island School of Design, Museum of Art.

Opposite: *La-La at the Cirque Fernando, Paris* 1878.
Oil on canvas, 116.8 × 77.5 cm (46 × 30¹/₂ in).
London, National Gallery.

'L'Etoile' (Dancer receiving an ovation)
and details (above and overleaf), *c*.1878.
Pastel, 60 × 44 cm (23⅝ × 17⅜ in).
Paris, Musée d'Orsay.

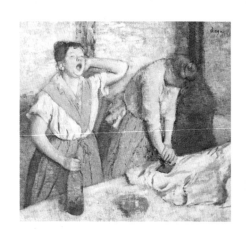

Women ironing, c.1884.
Oil on canvas, 76 × 81.5 cm (30 × 32 in).
Paris, Musée d'Orsay.

Milliner and detail (overleaf), 1885.
Oil on canvas, 99 × 109 cm (39 × 42⅞ in).
Chicago, Art Institute.

At the mirror and details (opposite and overleaf), c.1889.
Pastel, 49 × 64 cm (19¼ × 25¼ in).
Hamburg, Kunsthalle.

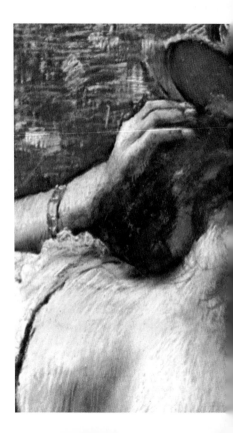

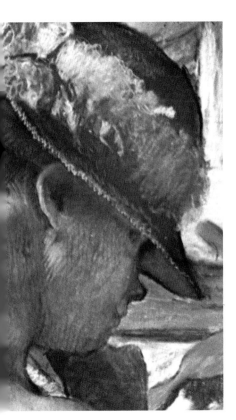

Above: *Before the rehearsal*, c.1880.
Pastel, 63 × 48 cm (24⅞ × 18⅞ in).
Denver, Art Institute.

Opposite: *Dancers backstage* 1890-1895.
Pastel, 65 × 70 cm (25⅞ × 27½ in).
Saint Louis, City Art Museum.

*Dancers behind the scenes, c.*1890.
Oil on canvas, 85 × 75 cm (33$\frac{1}{2}$ × 29$\frac{1}{2}$ in).
Paris, Musée d'Orsay.

Two dancers practising at the bar 1884-1888.
Thinned oil on canvas, 129 × 98 cm
(50¾ × 38½ in).
Washington, Phillips Collection.

Woman washing her left leg, c.1883.
Monotype and pastel, 19 × 41 cm (7½ × 16⅛ in).
Paris, Musée d'Orsay.

Above: *Woman drying her left foot, c.1886.*
Pastel on board, 54 × 52 cm
(21¼ × 20½ in).
Paris, Musée d'Orsay.

Opposite: *Woman combing her hair to
one side, c.1898.*
Pastel, 80 × 57 cm (31½ × 22½ in).
Paris, Musée d'Orsay.

The tub and details (opposite and overleaf), 1886.
Pastel on cardboard, 60 × 83 cm (23⅝ × 32⅝ in).
Paris, Musée d'Orsay.

Woman drying her neck and detail (opposite), *c.*1898.
Pastel on cardboard, 62 × 65 cm (24³⁄₈ × 25⁵⁄₈ in).
Paris, Musée d'Orsay.

Horse galloping on right foot, c.1882.
Brown wax with cork fragments on base,
height 41 cm (16⅛ in).
Geneva, private collection.

Horse galloping with jockey 1879-1880.
Brown wax, jockey's clothes of cloth, height
24 cm (9$\frac{1}{2}$ in).
Geneva, private collection.

Above: *Horse about to jump a hedge* 1879-1880.
Yellow wax, height 28.5 cm (11¼ in).
Paris, Musée d'Orsay.

Opposite: *Study for 'Little dancer of fourteen years'*, before 1881.
Red wax with dark spots, chalk base, height 72 cm (28⅜ in).
Geneva, private collection.

Above: *Grand arabesque, third position* 1882-1895.
Brown wax, cork and wood fragments in base,
height 43.5 cm (17⅛ in).
Paris, Musée d'Orsay.

Opposite: *Spanish dancer*, 1882-1885.
Green wax, height 40.5 cm (16 in).
Paris, Musée d'Orsay.

Above: *The tub*, c.1889.
Brown wax with zinc tub, chalk base,
height 47 cm (18$\frac{1}{2}$ in).
Berne, private collection.

Opposite: *Little dancer of fourteen years*
and detail (overleaf), exhibited 1881.
Red wax, black horsehair, waxed linen,
height 99 cm (39 in).
New York, Metropolitan Museum of
Art.

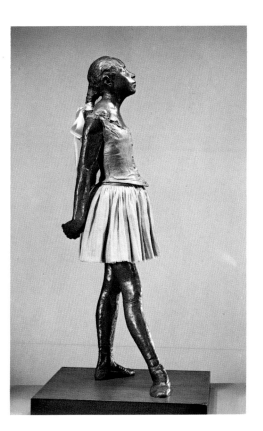

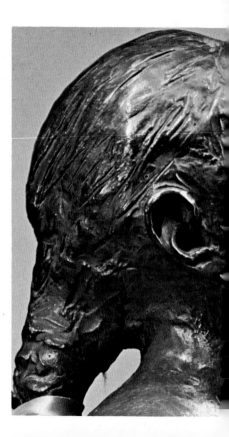

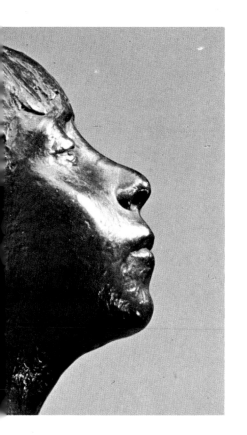

Geographical Index of Paintings

Berne, Switzerland
  Private collection:
  The tub (sculpture) 42
Cambridge, Massachusetts, USA
  Fogg Art Museum, Harvard
  University:
  Café-concert singer wearing a glove 89
Chicago, Illinois, USA
  Art Institute:
  Milliner 115-117
Denver, Colorado, USA
  Art Institute:
  Before the rehearsal 122
Frankfurt, West Germany
  Städelsches Kunstinstitut:
  Musicians in the orchestra 62-65

Geneva, Switzerland
Private collection:
Horse galloping on right foot 136
Horse galloping with jockey 137
Study for 'Little dancer of fourteen years'
139

Hamburg, West Germany
Kunsthalle:
At the mirror 118-121

Lisbon, Portugal
Calouste Gulbenkian Foundation:
Self-portrait saluting 42

London, England
Courtauld Institute:
Two dancers on stage 94-95
National Gallery:
*Young Spartans ('Petites filles Spartiates
provoquant des garçons')* 34-35
La-La at the Cirque Fernando, Paris 109

Lyons, France
Musée des Beaux-Arts:
The café-concert at Les Ambassadeurs 88

Minneapolis, Minnesota, USA
Institute of Arts:

Hortense Valpinçon 54-55
New York, USA
    Metropolitan Museum of Art:
    Woman with chrysanthemums 48-49
    Little dancer of fourteen years 143-145
Paris, France
    Musée d'Orsay:
    Absinthe 80-85
    At the races, gentlemen jockeys 86-87
    At the stock exchange 76
    The Bellelli family 43-45
    The cellist Pillet 60-61
    The dance lesson 66-69
    Dancers behind the scenes 124
    Dancer with a bouquet 104-107
    End of an arabesque 100-103
    'L'Etoile' (Dancer receiving an ovation)
        110-113
    Grand arabesque, third position 140
    Head of a young woman 50
    Horse about to jump a hedge 138
    Jockeys in front of the grandstands 46-47
    Marie Dihau at the piano 56
    Monsieur Perrot's dance class 96-99

The orchestra of the Opéra 57-59
Pagans and Auguste De Gas 51-53
A pedicure 71-73
Rehearsal of the ballet on stage 90-93
Self-portrait with pencil 40
Semiramis building Babylon 36-39
Spanish dancer 141
The tub (pastel) 130-133
Woman combing her hair to one side 129
Woman drying her neck 134-135
Woman drying her left foot 128
Woman washing her left leg 126-127
A woman with a vase 70
Women ironing 114

Philadelphia, Pennsylvania, USA
Henry P. McIlhenny Collection:
Interior 74-75

Providence, Rhode Island, USA
Rhode Island School of Design:
Dancer with a bouquet, seen from a loge 108

Saint Louis, Missouri, USA
City Art Museum:
Dancers backstage 123

Washington DC, USA

National Gallery of Art:
Achille De Gas in the uniform of a cadet 41
Phillips Collection:
Two dancers practising at the bar 125

Title Index of Paintings

Absinthe 80-85

Achille De Gas in the uniform of a cadet 41

At the mirror 118-121

At the races, gentlemen jockeys 86-87

At the stock exchange 76

Before the rehearsal 122

Bellelli family, The 43-45

Café-concert at Les Ambassadeurs, The 88

Café-concert singer wearing a glove 89

Cellist Pillet, The 60-61

Dance lesson, The 66-69

Dancers backstage 123

Dancers behind the scenes 124

Dancer with a bouquet 104-107

Dancer with a bouquet, seen from a loge 108

End of an arabesque 100-103

Grand arabesque, third position 140
Head of a young woman 50
Horse about to jump a hedge 138
Horse galloping on right foot 136
Horse galloping with jockey 137
Hortense Valpinçon 54-55
Interior 74-75
Jockeys in front of the grandstands 46-47
La-La at the Cirque Fernando, Paris 109
'L'Etoile' (Dancer receiving an ovation) 110-113
Little dancer of fourteen years 143-145
Madame Jeantaud at a mirror 77-79
Marie Dihau at the piano 56
Milliner 115-117
Monsieur Perrot's dance class 96-99
Musicians in the orchestra 62-65
Orchestra of the Opéra, The 57-59
Pagans and Auguste De Gas 51-53
Pedicure, A 71-73
Rehearsal of the ballet on stage 90-93
Self-portrait saluting 42
Self-portrait with pencil 40
Semiramis building Babylon 36-39

154

Spanish dancer 141
Study for 'Little dancer of fourteen years' 139
Tub, The (pastel) 130-133
Tub, The (sculpture) 142
Two dancers on stage 94-95
Two dancers practising at the bar 125
Woman combing her hair to one side 129
Woman drying her left foot 128
Woman drying her neck 134-135
Woman washing her left leg 126-127
Woman with a vase, A 70
Woman with chrysanthemums 48-49
Women ironing 114
Young Spartans ('Petites filles Spartiates provoquant des garçons') 34-35